P9-DBI-072

24 WORKING WITH AN AGENT

26 WHAT HOME, WHERE?

28 CONDO OR CO-OP?

30 EVALUATION CHECKLIST

32 MAKING YOUR CHOICE

34 MAKING THE DEAL

SHOPPING FOR A MORTGAGE

36 UNDERSTANDING LOAN OFFERS

38 WHERE TO GO FOR A LOAN

40 THE TWO MAIN KINDS OF MORTGAGES

42 OTHER MORTGAGE CHOICES

GETTING YOUR MORTGAGE

44 THE APPLICATION

46 THE MORTGAGE AGREEMENT

48 DOCUMENTS FROM THE LENDER

50 DISCLOSING ALL OF THE COSTS

52 MORTGAGE PAYMENTS

54 ADDITIONAL COSTS

BUYING YOUR HOME

56 TAKING TITLE

58 INSURANCE

60 HOME INSPECTIONS

62 PREPARING FOR THE CLOSING

64 AT THE CLOSING

66 UNDERSTANDING EQUITY

68 KEEPING INFORMED

70 INDEX

72 ACKNOWLEDGMENTS

INTRODUCTION

Buying a home has the potential to be one of the most rewarding, yet most stressful experiences of your life. With its simple explanations and straightforward organization, Buying the Best Home is designed to help you feel more in control by making the process easy to understand and smoother to perform. Without committing hours of your valuable time, you will learn the terms, tasks, documentation, and the insights to help you buy the best home for you. There are many ways to make home ownership a reachable goal. This book will guide you step-by-step through the home buying landscape so that your buying experience may be as satisfying as the experience of living in your new home.

BEFORE YOUR SEARCH BEGINS

Understanding the basics of home buying and
being prepared for all the steps involved will make
your search easier, faster, and more enjoyable.

VIEWING THE MORTGAGE LANDSCAPE

The process of securing a home mortgage may seem rigid and
invasive, but it's the thoroughness that makes it possible for
so much money to be available for home loans.

BORROWERS

Most home buyers need to borrow cash to pay home sellers in full. In the world of mortgages, a home owner's mortgage payments often become an investor's income. The lenders rarely meet the borrowers, so they rely on a system of detailed documentation to assure that you and the home you're considering are worthy of their investment.

LENDERS

Various institutions lend money for mortgages. Among them are mortgage banks, savings and loans, banks, and credit unions. Lenders may keep loans and profit from interest and fees, or sell loans to other investors, profiting from the up-front fees and monthly payments from the actual lender.

PACKAGERS

Huge financial institutions such as Fannie Mae (FNMA) and Freddie Mac (FHMC) (the two primary originators of home loans) are packagers. They buy loans from lenders (the ones you deal with), then either keep them or bundle them into large packages of $500 million or more. These packaged loans, called *mortgage-backed securities*, are sold with guarantees to large investors. In other words, if a home owner fails to repay a mortgage, the packager will pay the investors and take the loss.

LARGE INVESTORS

The large investors, such as insurance companies, pension funds, and mutual funds, buy the packages to earn the interest paid on mortgages. Investors come from all over the world because American homeowners are considered to be among the most reliable groups of borrowers in the world. In short, an investment in a mortgage-backed security is considered a relatively safe investment. The reliable stream of payments is a source of steady income, and helps these investors plan their cash flow.

SMALL INVESTORS

The large investors may attract small investors (people like you) by offering the prospect of sharing in the steady income and low-risk investments. One type of mutual fund, for example, is a Ginnie Mae (GNMA) fund, where the main portion of income earned comes from home mortgage investments. So, if you invest in an insurance policy or a mutual fund for its income, you may actually be receiving income paid from your own mortgage payments!

IT'S A FACT

New home sales in the United States in 1999 were between 850,000 and 950,000. Sales of existing homes were about 5.2 million during that same year.

TO RENT OR TO BUY?

W hen will you be ready to buy a home? What are the benefits and limitations? Considerations generally fall into two categories.

MONETARY ISSUES

Renting:

- Little or no maintenance costs;
- No down payment. Do need security deposit and possibly first and last month's rent;
- Can't lose money from falling home values;
- Moving expenses in and out;
- No tax breaks;
- No property tax;
- Rent can rise with inflation;
- Typically you get less space for the money.

Owning:

- Ongoing repair and maintenance responsibility;
- Down payment required, but for some, can be little or no money;
- Can gain value and be available as a loan resource (equity loan);
- Can also be a major resource for money during retirement;
- Can lose value;
- Moving expenses in and out;
- On-time payments build good credit record. Late payments significantly harm credit record;
- Significant tax breaks can make payments as low as renting;
- Property taxes, insurance, etc.

IT'S A FACT

The Consumer Price Index (CPI), which measures cost of living trends, includes the cost of rental housing in its computation.

A home may be good inflationary protection because most homes rise in value during inflation.

NON-MONETARY ISSUES

Renting:

- Easy to move out;
- Not many responsibilities;
- Time to judge a neighborhood before making a permanent commitment to live there;
- Less stressful than choosing a home;
- May be restrictions on noise, use, design, pets, children, etc.

Owning:

- Moving typically requires more thought and time;
- Continuous reponsibilities;
- Requires commitment to choice of home and neighborhood;
- Usually more control over home design and improvements;
- No restrictions on who occupies the home or how you use it (apart from any local ordinances);
- Pride of ownership.

A HOME OR AN INVESTMENT?

According to the National Association of Realtors, homes have tended to appreciate an average of 5% a year. Consider the impact that can have on your assets.

1. You buy a $200,000 home and put down $20,000 (10%).
2. The home appreciates 5% a year for three years to $231,525.
3. Aside from other costs, you've earned a 157.6% return on your investment in three years. Why so much? Your home cost $200,000, but you only invested $20,000. The $31,525 increase in value on that $20,000 works out to be a 157.6% return.

On the other hand, that huge return may not give you as much profit as you think. There may be a considerable amount of other costs that would reduce your return. For example, you will have paid some closing costs. You may also pay a brokerage commission to sell the home and take your profit. In the end, most experts agree that people should buy a home first to be happy living in it, and second, as an investment opportunity.

MOVE OFTEN?

According to the U.S. Census Bureau, first-time home buyers tend to move within five years. Second-time owners tend to stay between seven and eleven years. Many people own at least four homes in their lifetimes.

GOVERNMENT SUPPORT

Home ownership is encouraged in this country. When deciding how much home you can afford, be sure to factor in the financial assistance you will receive in the form of tax breaks.

GOVERNMENT SUBSIDIES

The government essentially subsidizes your monthly mortgage payments based on your federal tax bracket. For example, if you itemize on your tax return, you're in the 31% federal tax bracket, and your monthly mortgage is $1,500, you could pay $465 less in taxes and redirect it to your housing costs instead. So, in effect, your cost would be $1,035.

2 "Points" are up-front costs that are tax deductible.

YOUR TAX BRACKET	THE SUBSIDY
39.6%	39.6% of $1,500=$594
36%	36% of $1,500=$540
31%	31% of $1,500=$465
28%	28% of $1,500=$420
15%	15% of $1,500=$225

YOUR TAX BRACKET	YOUR ACTUAL COST
39.6%	$1,500-$594=$906
36%	$1,500-$540=$960
31%	$1,500-$465=$1,035
28%	$1,500-$420=$1,080
15%	$1,500-$225=$1,275

HUGE TAX EXCLUSION

If you sell a home that was your primary residence for at least two of the previous five years, the first $250,000 of gain ($500,000 for joint owners) is excluded from capital gains tax. You can sell a home and take the exclusion once every two years.

◀ ADJUST WITHHOLDINGS

To increase your take-home pay and take advantage of a tax break every month, ask your employer whether you can adjust the withholdings on your W-4 form by:

- *Taking allowances for each dependent you claim;*
- *Claiming yourself as "head of household;"*
- *Claiming dependent care credit.*

The worksheet on the back of your W-4 form gives you step-by-step instructions on how to calculate your allowances to include property tax payments and estimated mortgage interest.

MOVING AND INCOME TAXES

If you're moving at least 50 miles away because of a job transfer or a new job, many of your moving expenses qualify as tax deductions. A permanent change of station in the armed forces also makes expenses eligible for tax deductions. Expenses that qualify are:

- Packing and transporting household goods and personal items;
- Your car mileage to move items, yourself, and household members;
- Tolls and parking expenses related to the move;
- Storing and insuring items for up to 30 days;
- Disconnecting and connecting utilities;
- Shipping cars or pets;
- Transportation and lodging (but not meals) for all family members while traveling to your new home.

WHY GOVERNMENT SUPPORT?

Owning a home is good for the economy and society.

- Borrowing promotes worldwide circulation of money;
- Borrowing supports industries;
- The responsibility of a monthly mortgage promotes good work habits and productivity;
- Ownership promotes raising of families;
- Ownership promotes cleaner, safer neighborhoods.

HOW MUCH HOME CAN YOU AFFORD?

Your cash savings, monthly income, and credit record all factor into how much you can afford to spend on a home. This information is important to lenders as well as to you.

PURCHASE PRICE

IT'S A FACT

According to a study by the National Association of Realtors, in late 1999:

- The median price of an existing (not new) home was $133,300;
- An American family earning the median income could afford a home costing $173,400.

During the same period, the typical first-time buyer, earning $28,462, could afford a home costing $90,500.

DOWN PAYMENT

The down payment is the amount of the purchase price you pay for in cash.

More cash, smaller loan. The more cash you put down, the smaller your loan will be. So if you have a lot of cash but a low monthly income, you can make a large down payment, borrow less, and have smaller monthly payments.

Less cash, larger loan. On the other hand, if you have little cash but a high monthly income, you can buy a home with a small down payment and have a large loan.

CASH

Where will you get the cash? Here are some of the many possibilities:

- Cash in the bank;
- Savings and investments you can afford to sell;
- Valuables you wouldn't mind selling (it's like exchanging them for a bigger valuable, such as a home);
- Many 401(k)s and other retirement plans allow you to borrow from your account to raise cash;
- Gifts or loans from friends or relatives;
- Grants from non-profit groups, et al.

3 Some company retirement plans don't allow you to borrow for home purchases. Ask your benefits department.

MORTGAGE

The mortgage is your loan. Of course, the larger the loan, the larger your monthly payments. Each payment is actually two payments written as one check.
Principal. A portion of each payment repays the amount you borrowed.
Interest. The remainder of each payment goes to pay the interest on the loan.

MONTHLY PAYMENTS

How large could your monthly mortgage payments be?
Monthly income. Add up all your regular and recurring income that can be documented. Beyond income from work, include ongoing income from real estate, stocks and bonds, royalties, annual bonuses, and unearned sources of income such as alimony. Use a 12-month figure and divide it by 12 to get the monthly amount.
Monthly debt. Subtract from your total income the amount you pay in fixed debt, such as car loans, student loans, and divorce payments. You don't have to include a debt that will be paid off within six months. Credit card debt, unless very high, can be excluded, too.

OTHER COSTS

Many people don't consider (or prefer not to consider) all the associated costs of home buying. You will find information on all of these costs in this book. As an overview, you will probably pay:
- Closing costs, which you may be able to add to your loan amount;
- Mortgage insurance, if your down payment is small and the lender requires it;
- Home insurance;
- Moving costs;
- The cost of renovations;
- Monthly upkeep for services such as gardening, a pool, and for unexpected repairs;
- Utilities. They may cost more than in your current home.

SPECIAL ASSISTANCE

Depending on your income and financial situation, you may be able to receive financial assistance through one of several government-sponsored programs.

 4 Home equity can be a valuable resource for emergency funding.

THE LENDER'S CONSIDERATIONS

L *enders want you to take out a loan that's within your ability to repay. They have varying formulas to make their calculations, but they adjust their criteria depending on the amount of your down payment and the reliability of your income. Lenders look at the profile of the home as well as your profile because both are important in assessing their risk.*

5 Don't neglect repairs. Poor maintenance can cause your home to lose value.

HOUSING EXPENSES AND YOUR INCOME

Lenders consider how much your income can support. Your monthly housing expenses should be between 25% and 45% of your gross monthly income, depending on where you live.

LONG-TERM DEBT

Lenders consider all other long-term debts you're committed to repaying. Any debt that will take at least ten months to repay is considered a long-term debt. Keep in mind that your loan may not be approved if your monthly housing expenses combined with your total monthly debt is more than about 36% of your gross monthly income (or up to approximately 55%, in high cost areas of the country).

IF YOU'RE SELF-EMPLOYED

Buyers who are self-employed may need to provide lenders with:
- A year-to-date profit-and-loss statement (P&L);
- Tax returns from the last two years;
- A year-to-date balance sheet prepared by an accountant;
- Any contracts showing future income.

CREDIT HISTORY

Lenders are swayed by your credit history. Increasingly important is your *credit score*. It's a snapshot of your credit risk at a particular point in time. It can change regularly as information is added to your credit file. Credit scoring allows lenders to price according to risk. Borrowers with excellent credit may be offered lower interest rates. Borrowers with lesser credit may not be denied, but can expect to be offered loans with higher fees or more rigid terms to protect the lender from greater risk.

THE LOAN-TO-VALUE RATIO

Equity is important to lenders, too. Although they're not concerned about your profit, they do want to be repaid, earn a profit from interest, and avoid losses. So they look at the Loan-to-Value Ratio (LTV). This is the difference between the loan amount and the home's market value. So if the lender gives you a loan of $75,000 on a $100,000 home, the loan-to-value ratio is 75%. The bigger the difference between the loan amount and the home's value, the smaller the loan-to-value ratio. Some lenders are willing to finance loans as high as 135% LTV (loans larger than the home's value). The interest you pay on the amount over 100% of the purchase price isn't tax deductible.

MAKING A LOW DOWN PAYMENT

Sometimes, the only difference between renting and being able to afford to buy a home is the cash you have available for a down payment. In today's market, home buying can be within reach even for people with little or no cash, mainly because of mortgage insurance.

HOW MUCH DO YOU NEED?

Lenders historically have asked home buyers to put down at least 20% of the purchase price. The only way around that used to be special programs offered to veterans, first-time buyers, and others (see pg. 38). Today, however, you can buy a home with a 5% or 10% down payment. In rare cases, you may even make no down payment and still be able to borrow more than the purchase price. The biggest reason why low down payments are acceptable today has to do with mortgage insurance.

PRIVATE MORTGAGE INSURANCE

If you put less than 20% of the cost of the home toward your down payment, you may have to pay *Private Mortgage Insurance (PMI)*. This protects the lender in the event you default. You will pay a one-year PMI reserve at the closing, plus a monthly premium. PMI adds to your monthly payments. Typically, after you've repaid 20-25% of the value of your house, you may request that your PMI be cancelled. Ask your lender.

CREATIVE HELP

Even if you don't have much cash, a loan may not be out of your reach. There are many creative loan products designed to lower monthly payments on seemingly unattainable loan amounts (see pg. 42 for some examples). If you're going to stretch, though, be careful how far you go.

DOWN PAYMENT	YOUR OPTIONS
0%	Veterans with an honorable discharge may be eligible for a Veterans Administration (VA) loan. They also may pay lower fees and be eligible for a low interest rate. First-time buyers with a low income living in rural areas may be eligible for a government guaranteed loan. Many lenders also offer 0% down payments to borrowers with excellent credit.
3-5%	People meeting low-income requirements may be eligible for a loan insured by the Federal Housing Administration (FHA) or a loan through a state sponsored program. A lender may offer a 3-2 option loan, which allows 2% as a gift or grant for every 3% a buyer puts toward a down payment.
6-19%	This is enough to qualify for a conventional loan, buyers may have to accept slightly more expensive terms.
20% or more	Lenders believe that these buyers are those most likely to repay their loan. Because they are lower risk, these buyers are given better terms.

WHY PMI HELPS YOU

PMI doesn't directly protect you. It protects the lender in case a homeowner fails to make mortgage payments, a default occurs, and the home goes into foreclosure. The homeowner will lose the house and all the money already put into it. The lender is stuck trying to recoup the money it loaned. Mortgage insurance protects lenders against financial loss if a homeowner defaults, and in turn, helps more families buy homes by making it safer to lend money.

6 PMI must cancel automatically when your loan balance reaches 78% of the original home value.

▼ **BRIDGING THE GAP**
Even if you don't have a 20% down payment, that won't necessarily prevent you from buying the house you want. PMI acts like a bridge to help fill the gap between you and your dream.

PREQUALIFYING FOR A LOAN

Prequalification is a valuable, quick, easy, and free service from lenders. The process helps you assess how large a loan you could receive. Most of all, it gives you credibility with sellers. You're not obligated to take a mortgage from the lender who prequalifies you.

HOW IT WORKS

In some cases you can prequalify for a loan over the phone, in other cases you can walk right in and sit with a loan officer, who will ask you to estimate:

- The amount of cash you plan to use as a down payment;
- Your gross monthly income from all sources;
- Your monthly debt.

Based on the lender's current loan rates and fees, the loan officer will estimate what you can afford to pay for a home and the monthly payments, including mortgage, insurance, property taxes, and other expenses.

7 In high cost regions, lenders may allow housing costs to be as high as 45% to 55% of your gross monthly income.

HOW YOU BENEFIT

You benefit from prequalifying for a loan in many ways:

- You may find out you can afford more than you thought;
- When you tell home sellers you're prequalified, you gain instant credibility and have more leverage to bargain for a better price—the seller knows you can get the loan and close the deal;
- You can learn about a lender's loan requirements. For instance, some charge a penalty for paying off the loan ahead of schedule;
- You find out what other fees you may be required to pay;
- You find out if you have to carry life or disability insurance (this requirement is illegal in some states);
- You learn how much you need to deposit into a special reserve (escrow) account at the closing to cover taxes, home insurance, and other charges;
- You decide whether or not the lender is the right fit for you, which keeps you in control.

HOW LENDERS BENEFIT

Lenders benefit from prequalifying home buyers for loans because:

- They can begin to establish a relationship with borrowers. By knowing about your finances, lenders can target you in other marketing efforts;
- They have the opportunity to make you a customer. For example, a bank may have a program with lower costs for their own customers.

THINGS TO KNOW

Lenders are required to disclose certain information once you have applied for a loan. It helps to know at the prequalification stage:

- Your total cost of interest and fees over the life of the loan so you can compare different loans;
- The lock-in rate so you know what it would cost if you locked in at the current interest rate until closing;
- How many weeks it should take to process your loan.

March 22, 2000

Ms. Etta Johnson
Residential Brokerage Firm
555 Main Street
Anywhere, USA

Dear Ms. Johnson

Re: Kevin Smith

I am writing with regards to Kevin Smith's qualifications for the purchase of 5554 Canyon Road, Anywhere.

I can confirm that we have reviewed this transaction at length and that he is qualified to purchase the aforementioned property. This calculation was made assuming a down payment of 10% is made on the new home. I can confirm that I have reviewed the client's credit and received written ... of the necessary income

8 Get the prequalification in writing. The letter proves your credibility.

The Credit Report

Credit reports are provided by credit bureaus and are intended to be factual accounts of a person's borrowing and paying habits. Lenders use credit reports to verify the information provided by borrowers. You will want to check your credit report before you begin the buying process.

Ordering Your Report

Although there's a small fee, you're legally entitled to see your credit report—and to know how certain items got there. Many people order their reports before they apply for their loan, just in case they find mistakes or problems that could be resolved before a lender sees the report.

How to Dispute Information

Errors are inevitable. Have the credit bureau check out anything you think is wrong or requires further explanation. Send your request in writing and within approximately 30 days, the bureau will verify the information and send you the results. If you still dispute the report, you may include a written statement of 100 words or less in your credit file.

Who to Contact

Thousands of local bureaus are located across the country. They're all connected to at least one of three national credit networks that collect the data. You may contact them at:

Experian: 888-397-3742 (www.experian.com)
Equifax: 800-997-2493 (www.equifax.com)
Trans Union: 800-888-4213 (www.transunion.com)

Personal Identi
Mary Smith
555 Main St.
Town, State 99999

Credit Account Infor
Company Name
1st Nationwide Mortgage

Real estate mortgage
Conventional mortgage
American Express:
Credit card
Citibank - VISA
Countrywide
Real estate mortgage
Express
Charge
First USA Bank

A
am
Indiv
Individual
Individual Acc
Joint Account
Individual Account

IF CREDIT IS DENIED

You're entitled to a written explanation from the lender if you're denied credit. If your credit report is to blame, you're entitled to a free copy from the credit bureau, as long as you request it within 60 days.

COMMON ERRORS

Some common errors you may find in your credit report are:
- Confusing you with someone else who has the same name or a similar Social Security number;
- Failing to remove negative data after the issue is resolved;
- Failing to incorporate your comments into the credit bureau's file.

Call this number with questions -
Request Reference:
Report Date: 12 November 1999

CREDIT PROFILE

Social Security Number:
Date of Birth:

Date Opened	Last Activity	Type of Account and Status	High Credit	Terms	Items as of Date Reported Balance	Past Due	Date Reported
05/99	10/99	Installment Pays as agreed	$371K	$1935	$369K		
06/86	07/99	Open Pays as agreed	$0				10/99
/84	09/99	Revolving Pays as agreed			$0		10/99
04/99		Installment Pays as agreed	$410K	$2866	$1994	$0	09/99
95		Revolving Pays as agreed	$1000				05/99
		Revolving	$12000		$0		05/95
					$0		09/99

◀ **NEED HELP?**
You can contact a consumer organization, such as Genus Credit Management (www.genus2.org) or the National Foundation for Consumer Credit (www.nfcc.org).

9 Local credit bureaus may have information that doesn't appear on a national report.

Looking for a Home

People use a variety of tactics to find their homes.
Choices abound, and you are required to make
one decision after another. Here is some help.

Finding an Agent

Your home search can be frustrating. Finding the right agent
can help. Ask the right questions, look in the right places, and
you will find someone who can be a loyal partner in your search.

What Is an Agent?

The agent is a professional who can:

- Help you clarify your needs;
- Direct your search and focus your analyses;
- Arrange for you to tour homes (and go
  with you to view them);
- Negotiate in your best interest;
- Help you find financing and
  other services;
- Coordinate and manage all
  aspects of the transaction.

WHERE TO LOOK

There are many ways to find a good agent. You can:

- Get referrals from friends and colleagues as well as from your attorney or financial advisor;
- Interview agents at weekend open houses in areas where you want to live;
- Check the "For Sale" signs in the neighborhoods where you want to live for the names of local agents;
- If you're relocating, ask a local agent to recommend an agent in the new location (the agent may receive a referral fee from the new agent).

CHOOSING AN AGENT

It's important to choose the right agent for you—one who makes your needs a priority. Look for someone who:

- Makes you feel comfortable and confident, not anxious or pressured;
- Specializes in areas where you want to live;
- Returns calls promptly and answers questions readily;
- Informs you of new listings as soon as they go up for sale.

10 It may not be wise to buy a home (a very large investment) without the help of an agent or advisor.

CAPABILITIES CHECKLIST

Find out as much as you can about an agent before hiring him/her. Here are some important questions to ask:

- Are you a full- or part-time agent?
- Is your license in good standing? (Check with the state licensing agency.)
- Are you a broker and/or realtor? Brokers face more stringent licensing requirements and responsibilities. Realtors are voluntary members of the National Association of Realtors trade group and try to abide by their code of ethics.
- How many years of experience do you have? Experienced agents are best for the first-time buyer.
- Will you be working for the seller, too? If so, will you share any confidential information you give him or her with the sellers?
- How well do you know the area?
- Do you have an assistant? What does s/he do?
- Will you give me a list of homes you sold in the last year? If you're still not sure about this agent, ask for this reference list so you can contact some clients yourself and ask them about their experience.

Working with an Agent

G ood communication between you and your agent promotes the greatest chance of success in your home search.

Communicate Clearly

Before you begin the search for your dream home, make sure you and your agent are on the same page.

Set guidelines. Choose regular times to check in with each other and to view houses. Clarify your expectations and be sure you are both clear on what your agent will do for you.

Set your priorities. Save time by avoiding listings that don't meet your criteria. Clearly set your priorities with your agent.

Be opinionated. Be truthful about what you like and don't like about the house's condition, floor plan, and other specifications so your agent can find homes that meet your criteria.

Take advantage of your agent's tools. Ask your agent to let you know about properties that are about to be listed. Be prepared to drive by or visit a house on short notice.

If You Need Help

Always try to work out any disputes you have with your agent. Ask the office manager at your broker's office for assistance, if necessary. If all lines of communication break down and you think your agent has acted unethically, you can contact the local real estate board or a real estate attorney.

No Discrimination Allowed

Agents are prohibited by federal law from discriminating against buyers or sellers on the basis of race, color, religion, sex, national origin, handicap, or family status.

DIFFERENT TYPES OF RELATIONSHIPS

The type of relationship you have with an agent can affect how you interact with him/her. Be sure to discuss this before signing any agreement.

Buyer's agent. This agent works strictly in your interest and does not assist the seller in negotiations. In some states, you pay the buyer's agency commission (hourly, flat fee, or percentage of purchase price). In other states, the buyer's agent is paid by the seller.

Dual agent. In some states, agents can represent both buyer and seller (who must both agree to the arrangement). Typically, the seller pays the commission.

Transaction broker. In some states, you can hire a professional just to help both sides come to terms on the purchase contract. This person is more of a mediator or facilitator than a negotiator.

Seller's subagent. An agent may work for you and also work for the seller. This agency relationship means that your agent can legally pass on to the seller whatever information you provide.

THINGS TO KNOW

Many issues can arise in the home buying process that your agent can help you resolve.

- If you want to look in areas outside your agent's locale, s/he can refer you to another agent who specializes in that location. If you sign an exclusive contract with an agent, be sure it covers a short time frame and only the locations of that agent's expertise—not one that would keep you from working with another agent under any circumstances;

- If you discover that important negative information was concealed from you, your agent should know how to renegotiate or end the deal. Based on your state's laws, you may also have legal rights;

- It's unethical, and possibly illegal, for your agent to tell the seller or seller's agent how much you can spend on a home (apart from an offer)—unless your agent is also a sub-agent for the seller;

- Unless instructed otherwise by the seller, your agent must present all offers to the seller, even if s/he considers it to be too low. If the agent doesn't comply, you can speak to the agent's office manager.

IT'S A FACT

The buyer's agent and seller's agent typically split the total commission. A portion of their fees goes to their employers.

WHAT HOME, WHERE?

Searching for a home is an emotional activity. It's important that you start your search with clear priorities about what you want, both in a home and a neighborhood.

MAKE A WISH LIST

Think about what features you must have, would like to have, and don't need in your home. Be specific. For example, do you need an attached garage or do think it would just be nice to have one?

WHAT'S A BARGAIN?

Even if a fixer-upper, foreclosure, or other bargain may be your best bet for home ownership, consider these rules to help avoid buying a money pit:

- Look for bargain homes that need only minor repairs;
- Be sure the home has a good, basic floor plan;
- Always have the home and the property carefully inspected by a professional inspector before you buy;
- Estimate the repair costs before you commit to buying;
- Don't improve the home beyond the standards of the neighborhood.

STUDY THE MARKET

Your agent (and some Internet sites) can help you create a context for your home search. Here are some factors to consider:

Comparables. Actual, recent selling prices for comparable homes in the same area tells you if you are paying a fair price;

Median home price. Compare trends in home prices in your target areas over the last few years;

Sales during specific periods. Compare yearly and seasonal statistics to get a sense of different levels of market activity;

Average days on the market. Compare the length of time homes were for sale in a particular area during the previous few years. A high average may indicate a buyer's market or an area where homes don't sell easily;

Local job market. If the area in which you're planning to move is creating more jobs or high-paying jobs, the housing market will probably be competitive.

IT'S A FACT

1999 home sales set a record for the fourth consecutive year, with 5.2 million existing homes sold. This figure is expected to continue growing over the next few years.

RESEARCH NEIGHBORHOODS

If you're buying a home locally, drive around neighborhoods. Visit Open Houses to check out home values in the neighborhood. Whether you're buying locally or moving to another state, check the Internet for data on specific neighborhoods, including schools, crime statistics, median house price, number of homes sold, and any other information you feel is important to help you make your decision.

> **II** Keep in mind that selecting the right home almost always requires some compromise in what you would like to have.

RESALE VALUE

You may plan on living in your new home for at least the duration of your mortgage, but chances are you won't. So it's important to consider the home's potential resale value. Be sure you have all the facts and find out what the city has planned for the area. An expressway constructed a block away could drastically change your home's resale value. In some states, sellers are required to disclose signficant changes that could affect the home's value.

▼ **TARGETED APPROACH**
Focusing your search on two or three neighborhoods will help you master your understanding of those areas and keep you from becoming overwhelmed and confused.

CONDO OR CO-OP?

Owners of condominiums (condos) and cooperative apartments (co-ops) share common areas with other owners. These types of attached housing are affordable and popular choices of home ownership in today's expensive real estate market.

WHAT YOU OWN

You need to look closely at exactly what it is you own when you buy the various kinds of housing.

Condominiums. When you own a condo, you own an undivided interest in your unit (which, unlike a co-op, is real estate) and share ownership in the common areas. You pay an additional monthly fee that goes to common area maintenance. A townhouse is usually a condominium.

Cooperatives. If you belong to a co-op, it means you own shares in the corporation that owns the real estate, and you have the exclusive right to a single-unit apartment. In some cases ownership is similar to that of condos.

BUYING A CONDO

Be sure to read these documents, which you can get from the board of directors or a representative:

- The *bylaws*, which are the rules of the association, authorizing the board to assess fees, hire managers, and carry out other operation duties;
- The *house rules*, which state what can be done in common areas;
- The *covenants, conditions, and restrictions (CC&Rs)*, which spell out the private restrictions on the use of the property;
- The *purchase agreement*, which includes the right to inspect documents, and also includes financing and inspection contingencies that allow you to back out of the purchase.

12 The approval of the co-op board is required before any unit is sold.

BUYING A CO-OP

Before buying a co-op, be sure you have the answers to these questions:

- Are you allowed to see the sales records for the past year to check for rising or falling prices?
- What is the per unit value of the underlying mortgage?
- Are property taxes expected to go down or up?
- How are major repairs funded and are any planned?
- Is there an adequate reserve fund for repairs?
- Are there any lawsuits pending against the co-op?

RESERVE FUNDS

Read the financial statements and operating budgets to see whether the association has set aside a reasonable amount of reserve funds to cover unexpected expenses.

BUILDING EMERGENCIES

Reserve fund. The money collected each month from condo owners is used to pay for on-going expenses and set aside for emergencies in a reserve fund.

Special assessment. If the condo doesn't have a reserve fund, it can place a lien on owners' properties in the form of a special assessment. An unpaid lien can lead to foreclosure, so buyers should ask if special assessments are pending before signing on the dotted line.

THINGS TO KNOW

- Condos and co-ops are governed by a resident-elected board of directors. Residents are allowed to vote on issues depending on the rules of the association. Some associations weigh votes by the size of the voter's unit: The more square feet you own, the greater impact your vote has. Other condos simply allow each unit, regardless of size, one vote.
- Many condos restrict or ban rental units because they can reduce the value of all units in the building. If 30% to 50% of the units in a building are rentals, all the units may be considered investment property by lenders, which restricts buyers' financing options. Be sure you ask about rental policies before buying a condo.

EVALUATION CHECKLIST

The National Association of Realtors (NAR) has developed a way to compare and rate the homes you're considering to buy. Here is a checklist adapted from the NAR.

THE HOUSE—OVERALL

Total rooms:

Bedrooms _____

Bathrooms _____

Kitchen:			
Size	good _____	average _____	poor _____
Equipment	good _____	average _____	poor _____
Living spaces:			
Size	good _____	average _____	poor _____
Shape	good _____	average _____	poor _____
Ventilation	good _____	average _____	poor _____
Traffic flow among rooms	good _____	average _____	poor _____
Storage space	good _____	average _____	poor _____
Parking availability	good _____	average _____	poor _____
Level of property maintenance	good _____	average _____	poor _____

THE LOCATION

Commute to work	easy _____	average _____	difficult _____
Commute to schools	easy _____	average _____	difficult _____
Public transportation access	easy _____	average _____	difficult _____
Schools	good _____	average _____	poor _____
Stores	close _____	average _____	far _____
Hospital	close _____	average _____	far _____
Fire station	close _____	average _____	far _____
Police station	close _____	average _____	far _____
Public library	close _____	average _____	far _____
Place of worship	close _____	average _____	far _____
Post office	close _____	average _____	far _____
Parks and recreation	close _____	average _____	far _____

YARD
___ Level and well-drained ground
___ Smooth and not-too-steep driveway
___ Gardens and lawns well-established

FOUNDATION
___ No decay or mildew in basement
___ No rotting wood
___ Level slab that's not cracked
___ No big cracks in concrete
___ At least 6 inches of floor insulation

STRUCTURE
___ No major cracks or sags in the walls
___ Floors are level
___ Roof is in good condition
___ No water stains on ceilings or walls
___ Rafters don't sag
___ No damage to visible joints and beams
___ Attic ceiling doesn't allow light to shine through
___ Chimneys are in good working order

EXTERIOR
___ Doors aren't rotten; open and shut easily
___ Windows are weatherproof and not rotten
___ Paint is not peeling
___ Adequate gutters and drain pipes

13 Pay attention to practical details such as the square footage of the home and lot, average utility bills, and annual property taxes.

INTERIOR
___ House has been well maintained
___ Major appliances, including furnace, air conditioner, and water heater are in good condition
___ Floors don't sag or creak
___ Carpets are in good condition
___ Electrical wiring hasn't deteriorated
___ Electric service capacity is adequate
___ Circuits are not overfused
___ Kitchen and laundry room circuits are separate
___ Accessible outlets in every room
___ Water pressure is good
___ Waste water drains quickly
___ Plumbing doesn't make much noise
___ No plumbing leaks around joints
___ Toilets operate well

COMPARING TYPES OF HOMES

DWELLING TYPE	PROS	CONS
Single-Family Homes	More ownership	More responsibility
Condominium/Townhouse	Has services and amenities	Requires that you pay community costs
New Home	Less maintenance costs	Fewer choices in house style and neighborhood
Existing Home	An established neighborhood	Less expensive to live in; Higher maintenance costs

MAKING YOUR CHOICE

B*efore you make an offer on a house, be sure you know all the pros and cons, including the market conditions, all your options, and comparable properties.*

WEIGH YOUR OFFER CAREFULLY

Revisit your priority list and listing notes, and weigh all the factors carefully before you make an offer. Your purchase decision and your offer depend partly on:

- Your priorities ranked in order of importance so you can weigh which homes are the best match for the qualities you want;
- Comparable properties and how the homes that interest you stack up to other homes in the area. Ask your agent to prepare a comparative market analysis for you that lists and compares the prices of similar homes in the neighborhood that have sold in the past six months or are currently for sale;
- Market conditions and whether the homes on your list are in a buyer's, seller's, or stable market. Remember that houses in a seller's market may command higher prices;
- The pros and cons of each home. Review the notes you took while visiting each home and look for qualities that match your priorities. Some tradeoffs will be unavoidable.

14 Taking notes and even photographs of each home of interest will help you remember the details and make you more certain about your final decision.

THE COMPARATIVE MARKET ANALYSIS

Elements of a good analysis include the following items for a number of homes in the neighborhood you're considering.

Number of homes sold
Statistics on each home:
> Address
> Date sold
> Sale price
> Bedrooms/baths
> Square footage (home)
> Lot size (useable)
> Condition

Number of homes on the market
Statistics on each home:
> Address
> Date listed
> List price
> Bedrooms/baths
> Square footage (home)
> Lot size (useable)
> Condition

SELLER'S OR BUYER'S MARKET?

Understanding market conditions makes you a better buyer. In a seller's market, housing demand is high and supply is low so buyers often have to pay full price or more for their homes. In a buyer's market, housing demand is low and supply is high so buyers are able to negotiate.

MAKE YOUR CHOICE

Weighing all the facts will clarify what you are willing or not willing to accept while you're negotiating with the seller. Be sure you're clear on:

● What you must have, what you would like to have, and what would be nice to have but isn't worth the extra cost;

● What your overall pricing parameters are such as the highest and lowest price you will offer based on the realities of the marketplace and how badly you want the home.

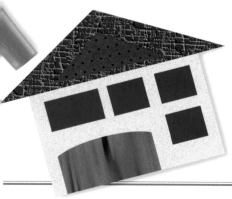

15 According to some sources, the average buyer looks at 10 homes before buying.

MAKING THE DEAL

The first step you take once you've found your dream home initiates a series of events. You make an offer to the seller, who either accepts it, rejects it, or makes a counteroffer.

1 OFFER

When you're ready to make an offer on a home, you will submit a standardized written purchase offer to the seller. The purchase offer is a legal document that specifies the price and any terms and conditions you request such as:

- Seller-paid termite inspection;
- Money paid by the seller toward closing costs;
- Appliances, window treatments, or any other items you want to specify as part of the conditions.

2 COUNTEROFFER

If there is an aspect to the offer the seller does not like, you may receive a written counteroffer stipulating the terms the seller prefers. You either can accept, reject, or make your own counteroffer. Counteroffers go back and forth until an offer is either accepted or rejected. If the offer is rejected, the sellers can't change their minds later on and hold you to it.

3 DEPOSIT

A deposit, called *earnest money*, is required when you make an offer to show that your offer is serious. Earnest money is used later as part of your down payment. Protect your earnest money by including a contingency clause in your purchase offer that requires the seller to refund the money if you can't get financing within a specified time.

CONTINGENCIES FOR CONDO BUYERS

Rules and regs. You may want to include a contingency that allows you to review the homeowners' association restrictions, bylaws, and budget, and to cancel the sale if the rules or finances are not up to reasonable standards.

Fixtures. Most purchase offers contain a paragraph about fixtures, which typically include wall-to-wall carpeting, major appliances, plumbing fixtures, built-in bookcases, and lighting. A good agent will make certain you've covered all the bases in your offer.

WITHDRAWING YOUR OFFER

In some states, you may be able to withdraw your offer up until you've been notified of acceptance. To avoid losing your earnest money or being sued, consult an attorney experienced in real estate.

4 CONTINGENCIES

Your purchase offer may include contingencies, which are a list of conditions that you're requiring before you agree to purchase the house. Some common contingencies are:

- If you cannot obtain financing from a lending institution, you won't be bound by the contract;
- A satisfactory home inspection report will be completed within a reasonable timeframe following the acceptance of the offer. If the report is not satisfactory, the transaction may be cancelled or renegotiated;
- Repairs or replacement of roof, carpeting, or appliances should be made;
- The seller provides you with clear title to the property.

5 BINDING OFFER

Only when either the buyer or the seller signs an unconditional acceptance of the other's terms does the contract become binding.

▲ THE PURCHASE CONTRACT

The purchase contract is the binding agreement between you and the seller. It should cover every aspect of the agreement, such as:

- *Legal description of the property;*
- *Sale price, payment terms, and amount of the deposit;*
- *Who gets the deposit if the the deal isn't completed;*
- *Type of deed, and seller's promise to provide clear title to the property;*
- *Target date for closing and a date when your offer will expire;*
- *Who pays for real estate taxes, utilities, title insurance, a survey, and termite inspections;*
- *Any state requirements such as the disclosure of environmental hazards;*
- *Your right to a pre-closing walk-through inspection;*
- *Any contingencies, such as the right to back out if you fail to secure a mortgage within a reasonable time.*

SHOPPING FOR A MORTGAGE

The type and terms of your mortgage may help determine how much house you can afford. You have many choices.

UNDERSTANDING LOAN OFFERS

Many people look at interest rates only when shopping for a mortgage because they don't understand the other aspects of the loan. But there's more than the interest rate to consider.

Mortgage Rate Report

Interest Rates for Purchases of Owners-Occupied, Single Family Homes

				Conforming Up to $203,150			Jumbo Over $203,150				
0-Year Fixed			TimesLine	Interest			Interest			Monthly	Maxi
der	Phone No.	Type	Access Code	Rate	Points	A.P.R.	Rate	Points	A.P.R.	Pmt. per $1,000	Loan A ($200
rrican Savings Bank	800-562-6272	S1	*2214	7.750	1.500	7.944	8.000	2.125	8.258	7.34	65
k of America	800-556-7811	B1	*2206	7.875	2.000	8.312	7.25	8.250	2.250	8.526	7.51	60
fornia Federal Bank	800-225-3337	S1	*2212	7.750	1.875	7.984	7.16	8.250	1.750	8.471	7.51	65
se Manhattan	800-586-2648	B1	*2217	NA	NA	NA	NA	8.063	2.500	8.364	7.38	1,00
se Manhattan Mtg.	800-900-6062	K3	*2226	7.750	1.625	8.142	7.16	8.125	2.250	8.399	7.42	3
ntrywide Funding	800-877-5626	K3	*2201	7.750	1.500	8.128	7.16	8.000	1.625	8.204	7.34	1,0
ney Savings & Loan	800-336-9639	S1	*2227	7.625	2.375	7.911	7.08	8.000	2.250	8.272	7.34	6
t Federal Bank of CA	800-672-4332	S1	*2208	7.625	2.125	7.884	7.08	8.125	1.625	8.330	7.42	4
t Mortgage Corp.	800-700-5650	K3	*2225	7.625	2.500	7.925	7.08	8.125	2.375	8.413	7.42	5

5-Year Fixed				Conforming			Jumbo				
erican Savings Bank	800-562-6272	S1	*2214	7.250	1.500	7.553	9.13	7.625	1.500	7.920	9.34	
nk of America	800-556-7811	B1	*2206	7.375	2.000	8.053	9.20	7.625	2.125	8.026	9.34	
ifornia Federal Bank	800-225-3337	S1	*2212	7.250	1.875	7.615	9.13	7.750	2.000	8.131	9.41	
ase Manhattan	800-586-2648	B1	*2217	NA	NA	NA	NA	7.563	2.500	8.027	9.31	*1,
ase Manhattan Mtg.	800-900-6062	K3	*2226	7.250	1.875	7.904	9.13	7.625	2.250	8.047	9.34	
untrywide Funding	800-877-5626	K3	*2201	7.250	1.750	7.882	9.13	7.625	1.750	7.962	9.34	*1,

◀ **A REFERENCE POINT**
Many newspapers show a table like this one every week. While the table may show outdated information (interest rates often change daily), you can gain a generalized sense of the current market. A mortgage broker can provide you with the latest data.

16 You can customize virtually any combination of terms you need.

Keep your cash . . .
Avoid up-front interest charges (points) you will pay as a fee to the lender. But expect a higher rate and higher monthly payments.

NO POINTS

| 6.56% FIXED | 7.07% APR |

LOW RATES
4.75%   8.20%APR

. . . or make low monthly payments.
Pay more points and you can lower your payments. If the APR is much higher than the interest rate, this may indicate that the lender is charging high up-front fees.

Stretch payments . . .
Spread them over the longest possible time (30 years). You will repay the loan slowly, pay much more interest overall, but each payment will be as low as possible.

30 Year Fixed
7.5% 7.85%APR
$6.99 per $1,000

15 Year Fixed
7.125% 7.5%APR
$9.06 per $1,000

. . . or repay quickly.
You will have higher monthly payments, but more of each payment will go toward repaying your loan. That means you will be building equity faster.

Take a chance . . .
Go for the lowest possible rate now and hope that rates don't rise substantially at each adjustment.

. . . or play it safe.
Get a rate you know you can afford now and you will be able to plan your future finances around it.

| 1 year adjustable 4.50% 7.41% APR | 3 year adjustable 5.87% 8.11%APR |
| 30 year fixed 7.31% 7.69%APR | 5 year adjustable 6.05% 7.91%APR |

NO INCOME VERIFICATION LOANS

Not much paperwork or many questions.
Consider this if you need to close quickly or can't prove you have enough income. But expect to pay for the privilege in up-front cash or a higher rate.

Term of the loan
The longer you take to repay the loan, the smaller each payment will be, but the loan will cost you more because you will owe more in interest. The less time you take to repay the loan, the higher each payment will be, but you will build your equity quicker.

Low Annual
30 year fixed
6.2% 6.85%APR
Hareison Federal Bank

Interest rate
Your annual fee for borrowing determines the amount of interest you will pay at each installment.

Annual Percentage Rate (APR)
A more accurate expression of your yearly cost of borrowing than just the interest rate, the APR takes into account the interest, points, and other costs such as credit report fee, mortgage insurance, and origination fees. Then these costs are spread over the life of the loan, which is usually fifteen or thirty years.

WHERE TO GO FOR A LOAN

*N*ow that you've found your dream home and you know more about your mortgage loan options, you can start shopping for your loan.

DIRECT LENDERS

Some direct lenders you can choose to shop at are:
Retail banks. Loan approval is often quick, rates are usually higher than average, and a larger than average down payment is often required. Retail banks lend their own money and set their own guidelines for approval;

Credit unions. They operate like retail banks but offer their services to their members only;

Mortgage bankers. Often affiliated with major corporations, mortgage bankers are solely in the business of selling mortgages. They set prices, process applications, fund closing costs, then sell loans to investors;

Insurance companies. Insurance companies often make large home loans. They may also allow their whole life policyholders to borrow against their policy's cash value at a low rate.

BEWARE HIDDEN OR EXCESSIVE FEES

Some lenders and brokers have hidden fees. What's more, the loan origination fee (essentially, the sales commission) may be unreasonably high. Be sure to shop around if your Good Faith Estimate (see pg. 49) shows it to be more than 3-4%.

THE GOVERNMENT

Federal Housing Administration (FHA). The FHA doesn't lend money, it insures loans meeting specific guidelines. The FHA insures lenders up to $208,800 (as of 2000) for loans on single-family homes. Home buyers pay the premiums, some up-front and some with the mortgage payments.

Farmers Home Administration (FmHA). The FmHA helps buyers in low-population areas get home loans. It also offers loans with strict guidelines to those who can't get a mortgage from a lender. The interest rate is based on what the buyer can afford and is guaranteed up to 90% of the overall loan amount.

Veterans Administration (VA). The VA guarantees loans to veterans of combat and some noncombat service. Veterans must have been honorably discharged to be eligible. If the buyer fails to repay the loan, the VA makes up some or all of the payment to the lender.

State programs. Many states offer special assistance for low income and first time buyers. The Department of Housing and Urban Development (HUD) provides support for low income housing and can guide you to special programs in your area. Call 800-245-2691 to find a program in your area.

OTHER SOURCES

You can shop for a mortgage with direct lenders, who:
● Have money to lend;
● Make the final decision on your application;
● Have a limited number of in-house loans available.

Or you can shop for a mortgage with mortgage brokers who:
● Are intermediaries that choose among many lenders;
● Have many lenders from which to choose;
● Are paid a fee based on the amount you borrow.

THE INTERNET

There has been an explosion of mortgage services on the Internet, both from brokers and direct lenders. Fees may be lower than non-Internet deals, but quality of service remains an issue.

THE TWO MAIN KINDS OF MORTGAGES

Home loans fall into one of two categories: fixed rate mortgages and adjustable rate mortgages (ARMs).

FIXED RATE

A fixed rate mortgage is the basic, straightforward loan that offers an interest rate that's fixed for the life of the loan. The same principal and interest amount is paid every month.

Variations. The standard length of a fixed rate mortgage is thirty years. But this can vary. You can own more of your home faster and pay less interest overall by paying off your loan in less than thirty years. The interest rate of a fifteen-year mortgage typically is .25% to .5% lower than the interest rate of a thirty-year mortgage. You can also raise or lower your monthly payments by paying points up front.

Once you've decided on the length of your mortgage and whether or not you will pay points, your payments remain fixed for the life of the loan.

17 Some ARM loans allow you to convert to a fixed rate loan at certain times for a fee or at a slightly higher rate.

PEACE OF MIND

Home buyers choose fixed rate mortgages because they know that their current income will cover the mortgage payments and their budgets can be planned reliably.

THINGS TO KNOW

You should consider an ARM if you:
- Can't afford payments on a fixed rate mortgage;
- Want to gamble that interest rates will eventually drop;
- Plan to repay the loan before it adjusts to the level of the current fixed rate.

TEASER RATES

Initial interest rates (*teasers*) are opening rates that are low to entice borrowers. Within the first few adjustments, the rates rise in line with current rates, and may leave you with payments you can't afford.

ADJUSTABLE RATE

As its name implies, an ARM is a loan that usually begins at a lower rate than that of a fixed loan and is adjusted periodically to stay in line with the interest rate trends of the economy. Lenders are legally required to give you information on how ARMs work. Each ARM has a formula that determines how much your rate will rise or fall over the life of the loan.

CONSUMER HANDBOOK ON ADJUSTABLE RATE MORTGAGES

Applicant(s) Name:

Property Address:

I hereby certify that Troxler & Associa has provided to all applicants the bool entitled Consumer Handbook on Adjus Rate Mortgages. This Booklet was d to all applicants within the require period

Loan Agent's Signature

Applicant(s) Signature

Applicant(s) Signature

CONSUMER
HANDBOOK ON
ADJUSTABLE RATE
MORTGAGES

▲ FULL DISCLOSURE

ARM borrowers receive the booklet, A Consumer Handbook on Adjustable Rate Mortgages, *and sign a document as proof of receipt.*

HOW ARMS WORK

Here is an example:

1. Determining the size of the adjustment.
How often. Payments adjust periodically. Typically, ARMs adjust every six months, or every 1, 3, 5, or 7 years.
When it occurs. The adjustment must be calculated before it's due to go into effect, typically 45 days in advance.

Find the index. Your loan is tied to the swings of another interest rate (or combination of rates), called the *index*. One common index is U.S. Treasuries (e.g., 1-year T-bills).	6.75%
Add a set amount. The lender adds a *margin* (the set percentage increase) to the index.	+2.50%
The adjusted rate.	9.25%

2. Limiting the adjustment
Every ARM has built-in protections.

Start with your current rate.	6.00%
Apply the cap. The cap is the most your rate can rise or fall at each adjustment.	+2.00%
Your new rate.	8.00%

3. Compare to the adjusted rate (from above).	9.25%
Hold at the cap.	-8.00%
The rate cap saves you.	1.25%

The ceiling. Also known as the lifetime cap, the ceiling is the most your rate can rise over the life of the loan. If your loan starts at 6%, for example, and the ceiling is 5%, your rate can never go above 11%.

OTHER MORTGAGE CHOICES

Besides deciding between the fixed and adjustable rate mortgages, home buyers are faced with other mortgage decisions. The more you understand mortgages, the smarter your decisions will be.

"NO DOC" LOAN

A feature in either a fixed or adjustable rate mortgage, no documentation loans offer a streamlined application process that requires fewer documents. Although the lender may not need such documentation as direct verification of employment, you're judged largely on your credit history, which must be excellent, and the size of your down payment, which could be large. This loan may carry a higher than average interest rate. Many self-employed people choose this option, especially if they can't verify a steady income.

BIWEEKLY MORTGAGE

Some lenders offer the option to make mortgage payments every two weeks rather than just once a month. This adds up to twenty-six payments (which actually makes thirteen monthly payments) over a one year period, as opposed to twelve. You save a lot in interest over the life of the loan and build up equity faster. You will need to be able to cover the faster cash flow to afford this type of loan.

GROWING EQUITY MORTGAGE

A fixed rate loan with a rapid payoff schedule, the growing equity mortgage is an inexpensive loan that requires your income to be able to handle flexible payments. Your payments will increase by a predetermined percentage, and the extra amount of each payment will be applied toward the principal portion of the loan.

18 The shorter the term of the loan, the larger your payments.

TWO-STEP MORTGAGE

The interest rate of a two-step mortgage adjusts only once, maybe five or seven years into the mortgage, then fixes at the market rate for the remaining term.

NEGATIVE AMORTIZATION LOAN

Aimed at buyers who need lower monthly payments, the lender basically fronts you some money to make your loan payments and gradually raises the loan amount to cover the additional loans. So over time you actually have less equity in your home as you make payments instead of increasing equity. This loan allows you to buy a house you could not otherwise afford.

SHORT-TERM BALLOON MORTGAGE

This mortgage may be attractive to buyers who expect to stay in their homes for only a short time. Payments are low and interest rates may be low because they're based on a thirty-year term. The full loan balance, however, is due before thirty years, typically in five or ten years. At that point you must make a balloon payment by paying off the loan or refinance your mortgage.

Balloon loans may be extendable. This means they have an extension feature that lets the lender make one adjustment to the initial rate for the balance of the years on the loan.

Some also have a feature that requires you to requalify if interest rates go up significantly before the rate adjusts. If you don't qualify, you will be forced to repay the loan immediately.

GRADUATED PAYMENT MORTGAGE

The interest rate and payments start artificially low in a graduated payment mortgage, so the loan is more affordable. Sometimes only part of the interest is paid and the remainder is added to the outstanding balance. This is known as negative amortization. This type of mortgage may also be obtained through a *buy-down* in which you pay points up front in exchange for the lower initial interest rate.

19 Balloon loans may be good for people who plan to live in a home only for a short time.

NON-CONFORMING LOANS

If you have a poor credit record, poor job stability, or other negatives, you may still be able to get a non-conforming loan. These loans are for high-risk situations so lenders will cover as much of their financial exposure as possible. Expect to make a larger down payment, depending on how poor your credit rating is, pay higher interest rates, high points, and fees.

GETTING YOUR MORTGAGE

After the contract is signed, it's time to apply for a mortgage. This stage can be much less stressful if you understand and are prepared for the process.

THE APPLICATION

Y*our loan application is often your only communication with those who may be willing to invest a lot of money in you. The longer it takes for you to be approved for a loan, the more likely something may go wrong such as interest rates going up or the property being damaged. So you will want to do everything you can to make the process speedy.*

Cash

HOW MUCH CASH? ▶
Mortgage lenders require home buyers to prove they have enough cash to cover the down payment (if any), closing costs, fees, and any moving expenses there may be. You may need to provide the lender with the past three to six months of every:
- *Bank statement;*
- *Brokerage account.*
Then lenders will verify your current and average balances for the last two to six months.

▼ HOW MUCH INCOME?

You will need to prove your ability to repay what you borrow by providing the lender with your last two pay stubs. The lender will verify your employment within the last two years and will ask your current employer about:

- *Any time you may have spent unemployed during that period;*
- *The likelihood of any pay raises;*
- *Consistency of bonuses, commissions, or overtime, if applicable;*
- *Likelihood of continued employment.*

Other income. You will want to provide your lender with year-end statements and other documents that prove:

- *Income from securities or a trust for which you will need to provide two years' tax returns;*
- *Social Security, disability, alimony, or child support only if you want it to be considered;*
- *A lease agreement to prove rental income, if applicable.*

THINGS TO KNOW

- Typically, you're allowed to borrow up to 50% of the amount vested in your 401(k) to buy a home. Amounts vary, however, from plan to plan. There's no set rule.
- A credit report fee and the appraisal fee are usually required when you submit the mortgage application.
- Relatives and close friends may give you a cash gift for your down payment, but you may need to prove that it's in your account and not a loan (because a loan would add to your debt).

◄ CREDIT HISTORY

Lenders will be looking at how you handle debt, and you will need to prove you've been a trustworthy borrower in the past. Your credit report will provide them with at least the following information.

- *Your credit card statements;*
- *Any open credit lines from lenders such as your bank;*
- *Any loans such as school or car loans and what you owe;*
- *Any legal judgments against you.*

Credit

Income

20 Even though it's possible to lose money and still run a successful business, most lenders want to see actual net income.

THE MORTGAGE AGREEMENT

*L*enders lay out all their terms in detailed legal language in the mortgage agreement. When you, the borrower, sign the agreement, you're promising to repay the loan. Four basic areas are covered in the mortgage agreement.

LOAN AMOUNT

The amount you borrow is called the principal. Usually, home buyers borrow the difference between the down payment and the sales price, but if you don't have enough cash to pay the up-front fees, some lenders will add that to the loan amount.

COST OF THE LOAN

The mortgage agreement will specify the:
- Interest rate you've agreed to pay;
- Total amount you will repay.

THINGS TO KNOW

- Most lenders allow you to make payments ahead of schedule, called prepayments. They may limit how much you can prepay or some may charge penalties. In many states, however, lenders are prohibited from restricting your prepayments.
- If you default on your loan and you owe more than your home is worth, your lender may sell your house, take the money, and reduce the principal owed to the sales price. This is called a short pay-off. The amount of the reduction is taxable to you. In some states, the lender may still be permitted to sue you for the difference.

21 Some states have notes and deeds of trust instead of mortgages.

EXTRA FEES

You will be charged a fee for bounced checks. You will be charged a late fee if your payment arrives more than ten to fifteen days past the due date.

REPAYMENT TERMS

A few factors go into how a loan is repaid.
Length of time. Is it a fifteen, twenty, or thirty year loan?
Frequency of payments. You repay the loan in installments. Are you making payments once a month or twice a month?
Variability. Are these payments fixed or will they be adjusted periodically? For adjustable mortgages, the agreement will specify if they are adjusted periodically, how it will be calculated, how much it can fluctuate up or down, what the minimum and maximum amounts could be, and when any adjustments will occur.

FAILURE TO REPAY

If you fail to keep your end of the bargain and default on your loan, your lender may force you to repay the full amount immediately or the lender may sell your home. Laws vary from state to state, but in general, you're considered to have defaulted on a loan if you:
- Are often over thirty days late with payments;
- Don't maintain your house, causing the property value to drop.

Lenders don't want to force you out of your home or be stuck trying to get back their money by selling (foreclosing on) your house. If you're honest with the lender, you may be able to arrange a compromise payment plan.

DOCUMENTS FROM THE LENDER

Lenders are required by law to give you information that explains your rights and what to expect from the loan.

LOAN DISCLOSURE

This form illustrates the workings of an ARM or other complex loan, if applicable.

> **22** Review your documents carefully. Don't wait until closing to resolve issues.

RATE LOCK-IN AND PROCESSING DISCLOSURES

The interest rate quoted to you when you apply for your loan may be different by the time you go to closing. Between the time of your application and the closing, you may want to lock in a rate you feel comfortable with. The Rate Lock-in Disclosure explains how much it will cost for you to lock in the current rate for various lengths of time. Compare this to the lender's Loan Processing Disclosure, which estimates how long your loan will take to process. Be sure your lock-in rate won't expire before you go to closing.

◀ **NON-DISCRIMINATION NOTICE**
Lenders are required to have you sign a statement that explains the law against discriminating on the basis of race, nationality, religion, or sex.

◀ **HUD SETTLEMENT BROCHURE**
This is an informational piece describing the services provided by your lender and the amount you will pay for them at closing. In most states, closing agents typically provide an estimate of closing costs a few days prior to closing. In states with escrow closings, where you don't go to an actual closing, you will receive the final statement after you close.

COMPLAINTS

Applying for a home loan and the closing which follows is a highly regulated transaction. Congress passed the Real Estate Settlement Procedures Act (RESPA) as a consumer protection statute designed to help consumers be better shoppers in the home buying process. More information about your rights under RESPA is available online at: www.hud.gov/fha/res/respa_hm.html.

TRANSFER OF LOAN SERVICING DISCLOSURE

Lenders often transfer the servicing of their loans to another company. The servicing disclosure form stipulates that you will be notified by both the lender and the new company usually within fifteen days of the transfer. You must be provided with toll-free numbers for both companies.

IT'S A FACT

Favorable weather tends to increase home sales, as it makes buyers more available to go out on home searches—and makes homes show in a better light.

THE APPRAISAL

An *appraisal* is an estimate of the value of your home that lenders use to determine whether the value is high enough to justify the loan. In many states you can request, in writing, to see a copy of the appraisal.

23 Within 60 days of a loan servicing transfer, any payment you make accidentally to the previous lender may not be treated as a late payment.

◄ GOOD FAITH ESTIMATE OF CLOSING COSTS
Also known as settlement costs, the good faith estimate of closing costs is not a guarantee because costs are subject to market changes. Because you must receive this estimate from your lender within three business days after you've applied for a loan, some lenders include the estimate in their application kits.

DISCLOSING ALL OF THE COSTS

Every lender or loan broker must give you a Federal Truth-in-Lending Disclosure Statement. You should receive this document very soon after you apply for a mortgage. The law requiring lenders to provide it was created to help people compare the cost of the loan against the cost of loans from other lenders they might be considering. While it's designed to present your true costs in simplified fashion, many people find it confusing. Here's what it tells you.

Finance Charge
This is the cost of the loan expressed in dollars. It includes the total amount of interest you will pay over the full life of the loan (in this case, 30 years), prepaid finance charges, and the total amount of mortgage insurance charged over the life of the loan.

Annual Percentage Rate (APR)
The APR is the actual cost you will pay on the loan each year (expressed as a percentage of the amount you borrow). The APR is always higher than the interest rate because it takes into account the fees and other costs, such as the upfront points, that you pay to get the loan. Since fees vary from loan to loan, the APR gives you a standardized number to use as a comparison.

Number of Payments
This tells you how many payments you would make if you kept the loan for its full length. In this case, the loan is for 360 months, which equals 30 years.

Amount of Payments
This is the amount you would pay each month. The single amount tells you that this is a fixed rate loan, where the payment amount doesn't change. If this were an adjustable loan, there would be a longer list of payment amounts to help you see how payments would change.

Demand Feature
When this box is checked, it means that the lender can demand full repayment if you default on the loan.

Late Charge
This tells you that, in this case, if your payment is received more than 15 days late (after the 15th of the month), a late fee of $34.96 will be added to your next month's bill. The "5" following the slash tells you that the fee represents 5% of the overdue amount ($699.22).

FED AL T

Lender/Broker: Troxler & Assoc

Borrower:

Property Address:

[X] Initial disclosure at time of application

ANNUAL PERCENTAGE RATE The cost of your credit as a yearly rate	FINANCE CHARGE The dollar amount the cr will cost you assuming no annual percentage rate of not change
E 7.818 %	$ 154758.

Your payment schedule will be:

NUMBER OF PAYMENTS	* AMOUNT OF PAYMENTS	
360	699.22	0

* includes mortgage insurance premiums, excludes taxes, hazard

[X] DEMAND FEATURE: This loan trans
[X] REQUIRED DEPOSIT: The annual p
[ ] VARIABLE RATE FEATURE: Your
have

SECURITY INTEREST: You are giving a
[X] the goods or property being purchased.
[ ]
FILING OR RECORDING FEES $ 75
LATE CHARGE: If a payment is more tha
principal and interest past due.
PREPAYMENT: If you pay off your loan ea

Amount Financed
It's the loan amount you applied for, minus the prepaid finance charges. It's lower than the amount you requested because the prepaid finance charges are deducted from the amount you borrow before the check is written. In short, this is the amount of the check the lender writes. In this case, the loan was for $100,000 and the amount received was $96,960. The remaining $3,040 covered the cost of the prepaid finance charges.

WHAT ARE PREPAID FINANCE CHARGES?

These include items paid at or before the closing, such as loan origination fees, lock-in fee, discount fee (points), adjusted interest, and the initial mortgage insurance premium.

Total of Payments
This represents the total amount you will pay if you make the minimum payments on time for the life of the loan. This includes principal (the amount borrowed), interest, and insurance premiums. It doesn't include property taxes or property insurance premiums. In this loan, $100,000 was borrowed and it will cost $251,719.20 to repay it in full one month at a time over the 30 years.

Total Sale Price
This amount is left with an "E" because the lender isn't accounting for the sale price of the home, only the amount borrowed.

When Payments Are Due
This tells you that payments are due on the first of every month beginning on June 1, 2000.

Required Deposit
When this box is checked, it means that your down payment isn't included in any of these calculations.

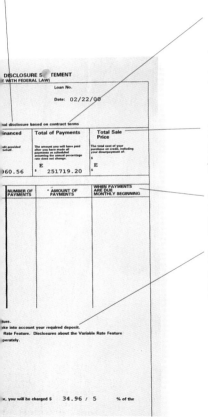

WHAT IS THE "E"?

The "E" on this disclosure means that these numbers and dates are estimates. The true cost will be known when you're ready for the closing.

MORTGAGE PAYMENTS

Your mortgage payments are determined by points, interest, and the term. By varying these options you can see how different types of loans play out.

30-YEAR FIXED RATE LOAN

What if you wanted to pay as little cash each month as possible and have payments stay the same for the life of the loan? You would choose a loan with a long payoff schedule, such as the traditional 30-year fixed rate mortgage. You might start, for example, with a $100,000 loan and an 8% interest rate fixed for 30 years. Your monthly payments would be $734 and the total interest you would pay (in addition to repaying the principal) over the entire term of the mortgage would be $164,155.

ONLINE CALCULATORS ▲
You can conduct an unlimited number of "what if" scenarios to see just how much any home loan would cost you. Simply go on the Internet, type in keywords such as "mortgage calculator," and see how many sites will do the work for you.

THE CROSSOVER POINT ▼
There is a point with every loan where you begin paying more principal than interest each month. With this 30-year loan it's the 257th payment and with this 15-year loan it's the 72nd payment.

Payment	1st	60th	84th	257th	Last
Interest	$667	$635	$617	$366	$5
Principal	$67	$99	$116	$367	$729

Note: Principal and interest amounts are rounded to the nearest dollar for simplicity.

15-YEAR FIXED RATE LOAN

What if you make larger payments each month but pay off the loan in far less time? For one thing, lenders usually will offer a lower rate for a quicker payoff period. For another, you will pay much less in interest over the life of the mortgage. Here, you begin with a $100,000 loan, and a 7.6% interest rate on a 15-year fixed mortgage. Your monthly payments would be $932.70 (higher than the 30-year loan) and the total interest paid would be $67,887 (much lower than the 30-year loan).

THINGS TO KNOW

- In most cases, you will pay much more in interest than principal during the early years of the loan.
- The average buyer either sells or refinances the home within five to seven years so no matter what your plans, consider how much you will have paid off at that point.
- Pay attention to the total interest you will pay over the life of the loan.

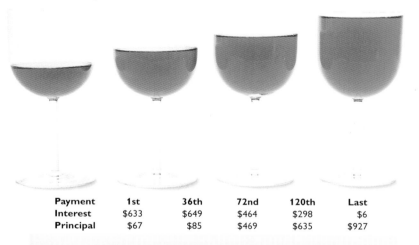

Payment	1st	36th	72nd	120th	Last
Interest	$633	$649	$464	$298	$6
Principal	$67	$85	$469	$635	$927

DRAMATIC SAVINGS POTENTIAL

Paying more than is required every month or making even just one extra payment a year can save you a lot of money. This prepayment of your loan is easy to do. It may be as simple as including extra money with one of your payments and designating it according to your lenders instructions, as an additional principal payment. Be sure your lender doesn't charge fees for prepayments.

ADDITIONAL COSTS

B *e sure you're prepared for the many expenses involved in buying a home. Costs are usually around 2% of the loan amount. Keep in mind that some of the fees you pay when you apply for a loan are not refundable.*

COSTS WITH THE LOAN APPLICATION

- The origination fee is either a percentage of the mortgage or a flat fee that may be included in the points;
- The credit report fee pays for the credit reports compiled for everyone who is responsible for repaying the loan;
- The application fee pays for processing the mortgage application;
- The appraisal fee pays for an appraiser hired by the lender to estimate the value of the home;
- In some cases there is, a survey or title search.

24 Many costs related to closings are tax deductible. Ask your tax advisor for assistance.

25 Depending upon where you live, the seller may pay some of the costs listed here.

COSTS THAT BENEFIT YOU

You may find it beneficial to order:

A home inspection. In addition to inspections required by the lender, you may want to protect yourself by making the sale dependent on satisfactory completion of a home inspection;

Owner's title insurance. A thorough title search can ensure a clear title. You still may want to purchase title insurance to avoid owing loan payments on property if ownership is disputed. Lenders, in fact, require separate title insurance to cover their interest;

An additional appraisal. If you're unhappy with your lender's appraisal of your home, you may want to request a second appraisal (at your cost).

Costs

Closing agent. Money goes into your escrow account, which holds and distributes certain payments when they become due. Your lender will have estimated these costs at the time you submit your application.

- You will pay your prorated share of any annual taxes due, such as property tax, school tax, and municipal tax into escrow for the remainder of the year;
- Your impound account pays the monthly premiums for private mortgage insurance (PMI) until you owe less than 80% of the value of your home;
- Most lenders require that you prepay the first year of homeowner's insurance and bring proof of payment with you.

The government. The government also charges fees.

- Recording fees go to the county clerk, who files the deed and changes the property tax billing information;
- Transfer or mortgage taxes are required in some places to transfer the title and deed from the seller to the buyer. Other state and local fees may apply.

The seller. The seller receives reimbursements, which pay for a prorated share of the property taxes and some services, such as trash collection.

The lender. The lender receives points, if any, each of which amounts to 1% of your loan. You can finance points with some lenders, adding the cost to your monthly payments. The seller must pay points for FHA and VA mortgages.

Third parties. Here are very generalized costs which vary from place to place.

- The title search may cost from $100 to $1,000. Title insurance is a one-time premium that varies in cost based on the value of the home;
- Your attorney fees may cost a percentage of the loan, flat fee, or hourly rate, and the lender's attorney's fees may cost between $200 and $500;
- The amortization schedule, which shows you how much you've paid at any given time, may cost $50 to $75 to prepare (not required but helpful);
- Inspections such as termite inspections that may cost from $200 to $300;
- You will be required to prepay the interest on your loan for the remaining days of the month.

BUYING YOUR HOME

You have chosen a home, selected a mortgage, and been approved for a loan. Now you need to make some decisions that will affect the ongoing ownership of your home.

TAKING TITLE

Each of the various ways you can take title to a house have legal, tax, and estate planning ramifications. Consider your options carefully and get expert legal advice if you need help.

WHAT IS TITLE?

Title is the term for ownership. The person or people whose name(s) appear on the deed is (are) the only legal owner(s).

DOCUMENTS OF ▶ OWNERSHIP

The grant deed is the document that's recorded to show who is the legal owner of the property. The title insurance policy is your proof that the ownership is transferred to you free and clear, and that no one else claims ownership in the property or is owed money that could be paid by selling the property.

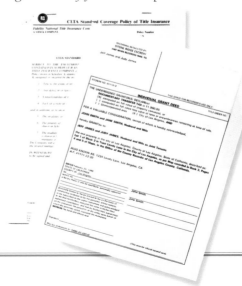

JOINT TENANCY

In joint tenancy with rights of survivorship (JTWROS), two or more people each own an equal, undivided interest in the property. This is the way married couples typically own the marital home. When one joint tenant dies, his/her share automatically goes totally to the survivor(s), no matter what the deceased joint tenant might have said in his/her will. This means that property passing from one joint tenant to another doesn't go through probate proceedings. For the home to be sold, all joint tenants must agree to the sale and sign the deed.

TENANCY IN COMMON

Two or more people can hold title as equal or unequal tenants in common. Each co-tenant owns his or her proportional share absolutely, and has the right to dispose of that property interest in any way or at any time. Unlike a joint tenancy, when a tenant in common dies, the ownership interest becomes part of his or her estate, and is subject to the provisions of his or her will.

SOLE OWNERSHIP

A sole owner owns 100% of the property in his or her name and is the only name on the title.

LIVING TRUSTS

A living trust can spare your heirs probate costs and hassle. For real estate to be placed in a trust, there must be a formal property transfer and a deed must be recorded. For example, the transaction might be from "Mom & Pop Jones" to "Mom Jones & Pop Jones, Trustees of the Jones Family Trust, under a trust agreement…" First, talk to your mortgage lender and ask how to handle it. Most lenders are used to dealing only with corporations or individuals, but most will allow the title to be held by the trust when they realize this doesn't reduce your personal responsibility for the mortgage debt. If, however, you say nothing and take title as joint tenants with your spouse, for example, a later transfer of the property into a trust may trigger the "due on sale" (repay in full) clause that's probably in your loan agreement. Be aware, though, that if you want to refinance property in a living trust, you may have to transfer title out of the trust.

COMMUNITY PROPERTY

In community property states (e.g., California and Texas) it's presumed that each spouse has a 50% interest in all property acquired during the marriage, including the home. The property interest of a deceased doesn't automatically pass to the survivor at death. That result can be accomplished, however, by the deceased's will.

INSURANCE

*B*efore buying a home, figure in the cost of insurance. How much and what types of insurance you need are important decisions for you to make when buying a home.

THE STRUCTURE OF YOUR HOME

You can insure the structure of your home in three ways:

Replacement cost. This is capped at a maximum dollar figure and pays the cost of replacing damaged property;

Guaranteed replacement cost. Not available everywhere, this insurance has no dollar limit, and pays the full cost of replacing damaged property. Some companies limit the coverage to 120% of the cost of rebuilding your home;

Actual cash value. This insures the home for the amount equal to the replacement value of damaged property minus depreciation.

PERSONAL BELONGINGS

You have many options when insuring your personal belongings.

Casualty insurance. Protects you against losses to your property due to theft, vandalism, fire, and weather-related damages. You need to get casualty insurance to close on your mortgage.

Personal property. This insurance covers all your furniture, jewelry, clothes, and other personal items, usually for up to 50% of your structural coverage.

THE RIGHT COVERAGE FOR YOU

Consider insuring your home for the total cost of rebuilding it. Calculate the cost by multiplying the building costs per square foot by the total square footage of your house (consult your local builders association). Keep in mind that the type of structure, the number of rooms, the type of roof, and special features all affect the cost of rebuilding a home. Don't insure your home for its market value because the cost of rebuilding may differ from the price you paid or the price you could sell it for today.

PERSONAL INJURIES

You can also protect yourself from personal injuries. Liability insurance protects you in the event you're sued by someone injured on your property. People may try to sue you for their injuries which occur on your property, whether they were invited or uninvited guests.

REDUCING THE RATE

Depending on the company, homeowner's insurance can vary by hundreds of dollars. You can reduce the rate you pay by:

- Researching companies for discounts, including buying your home and auto policy from the same insurer;
- Raising your deductible;
- Installing smoke and fire alarms that warn an outside service;
- Insuring just your home, not your land;
- Buying group coverage, if possible;
- Staying with the same insurer—you may be rewarded with a lower premium after three to five years;
- Adjusting your policy annually to cover any major additions or purchases;
- Removing items from your home which may be a hazard, such as exterior masonry work if you live in earthquake country.

OTHER INSURANCE TO CONSIDER

You may want to buy additional insurance such as:

- Loss of use insurance (usually 10-20% of your structural coverage) provides living expenses when you can't live at home;
- Umbrella liability insurance provides one policy that covers both your home and car, and may increase liability coverage on both;
- Most insurance policies cover wind, hail, and other weather conditions. But in areas susceptible to catastrophic losses from nature such as hurricanes and earthquakes, you will probably need to buy additional coverage.

CO-OP AND CONDO INSURANCE

Co-op and condo owners need two separate policies. The master policy is provided by the co-op/condo board and covers the common areas such as the roof, elevator, and walkways. Be sure you know what's covered by your building's association. Your own insurance policy covers your personal belongings, structural improvements, liability, and living expenses in the case of fire, theft, or other disaster that's listed in your policy.

HOME INSPECTIONS

Having your potential new home inspected is one way for you to protect your interests. Your purchase agreement should allow you to cancel the deal if you're not satisfied with the inspection.

WHAT IS A HOME INSPECTION?

A complete inspection usually costs $175 to $500 and includes an examination of all of the home's main structures and systems, such as the home's foundation, windows, wood in the structure and window sills (which is checked for signs of rot or similar damage), plumbing, electrical, heating, air conditioning, and built-in appliances. Some inspectors also offer a check for radon gas and lead in the paint and pipes.

WHY HAVE A HOME INSPECTION?

When your house is inspected, you should get a thorough report of the inspector's findings. Sometimes photographs accompany the report. You can use this report to:

- Identify defects that could have an effect on your negotiations;
- Avoid buying other people's problems that could cost you a lot of unexpected expenses;
- Identify hazardous conditions;
- Save you the money and time that would be required for you to get the house to meet your standards.

26 A home warranty is an inexpensive way to protect yourself against problems that may occur despite the home inspection.

27 It's a conflict of interest for the inspector to offer to repair anything for an additional fee.

SOME ITEMS ON AN INSPECTOR'S CHECKLIST

Here are some of the most common items on an inspector's checklist. S/he will check to see that:

- Water drains away from the building and isn't allowed to stand near the foundation;
- Tile grout in the bathroom is sealed so water doesn't damage it;
- The toilet wax rings prevent leaks;
- The attic is well ventilated to protect your roof and keep water from condensing on the insulation;
- Your furnace was properly maintained;
- There is at least six inches between the wood of your house and the soil to keep water from entering your home;
- There aren't any inordinate or unusual cracks in your concrete foundation that might be an indication of instability;
- All accessible electrical wiring is safe and and properly installed.

28 You can get a checklist from an inspection association.

IMPORTANT CRITERIA

All states require engineers be licensed, but may not require licenses for home inspectors. It helps, therefore, to hire a home inspector who is appropriately credentialed and experienced. You should also expect any home inspector you select to:

- Be insured;
- Provide you with a detailed, written, and timely report;
- Be affiliated with a state or national home inspection association or oganization, such as the American Society of Home Inspectors.

THINGS TO KNOW

- If possible, be there for the home inspection (around two hours). This is a great time for you to ask questions and learn more about your new home.
- Since there will be a gap of time from the date you sign your purchase agreement until your closing, have your house inspected again and try to do another walk-through the day before the closing.
- You might want to buy a warranty that protects you in case the inspector misses anything.

PREPARING FOR THE CLOSING

The more informed you are, the better off you will be when it comes time for your closing. Several people get involved in every closing, so use this checklist to help you stay on top of things.

IN ADVANCE

Organize the tasks required for closing.

__Order an insurance binder to prove you've insured the home;

__Decide how you want to take title and tell your escrow holder;

__If you've hired one, make sure the moving company is ready to move you on the proper date or reschedule if your closing has been delayed;

__Mail change-of-address cards, which you can get at any post office;

__Notify the post office to forward your mail;

__Disconnect your current utilities and make sure you are refunded any deposits you may have made;

__Order all of the utilities to be turned on in your new home;

__Find out from your lender if one of its representatives needs to be present when you sign the final loan contract.

POWER OF ATTORNEY

If a co-owner can't make it to the closing, be sure you have a notarized and signed power of attorney from him or her, giving you the authority to sign in his or her absence.

IT'S A FACT

Here are some average home prices in the United States from January, 2000:
Nationwide: $168,800
Northeast: $170,400
Midwest: $144,100
South: $148,800
West: $228,000

Source: National Assoc. of REALTORS®

BEFORE CLOSING

__ Conduct your final walk-through. Keep in mind you can delay the closing if the necessary repairs haven't been made or if you see any unauthorized changes;

__ Review your estimated settlement statement to see whether it reflects your closing fees accurately. If something doesn't look right, call your closing agent for an explanation and take steps to have the problems corrected, if necessary;

__ Deposit into your checking account the cash you need for closing;

__ Call your closing agent to ask for a list of what you need and to confirm the time of your closing.

TO DO: YOUR AGENT

Your agent will schedule the inspections, help solve any problems, and make sure everything is taken care of in time for the closing.

TO DO: YOUR LOAN REP OR MORTGAGE BROKER

This person will process the loan application, secure the financing, and provide the loan so the sale can be completed.

ON CLOSING DAY

Procedures vary from state to state so be sure you know exactly what to expect in your state (in some states, some of the following may be done ahead of the closing day).

__ Bring a certified check for the down payment. If you've deposited your down payment in escrow, the holder will have the certified check for the seller;

__ Bring separate checks to pay for various closing costs;

__ Bring your checkbook to pay any small unexpected costs;

__ Bring a copy of important papers such as your purchase agreement, estimate of closing costs, and a binder for home insurance from your insurance company.

AT THE CLOSING

In most states, you go to an actual closing, where everyone is paid and protected. But in some states, there are no face-to-face closings. Instead, closings are handled by mail or through an escrow agent.

MONEY IS DISTRIBUTED

Now it's time to see all your diligence and hard work actually purchase your home. At closing, money is paid to various people.

To the lender. You pay the points and fees to your lender. Your first regular mortgage payment begins at the end of the following month because each payment covers the previous month, but interest on the loan begins right away.

To the seller. You pay any down payment remaining, any other agreed-upon expenses, and any adjustments for monthly gas and electric bills.

To an attorney or escrow account. You put money into an escrow account, held by the lender, which assures your lender that certain future bills will be paid. This money gets distributed to the proper places when bills are due.

DOCUMENTS ARE SIGNED

Your representative should review each document carefully and explain its significance to you before asking you to sign it. Here are some of the things you will be asked to do:

- Promise to repay the loan. If you fail to repay your loan, the lender is authorized to sell your home to recoup the money;
- Clear up any last minute credit issues that show up against you. A search may also uncover claims against someone else with your name or similar Social Security number and you will be asked to verify that these claims were not against you;
- Receive the official document that transfers ownership from the seller to you.

29 Many of the payments made at closing require a check guaranteed for payment by your bank, such as a cashier's or bank check.

THINGS TO KNOW

- If the seller owned the home for only a few years, the seller's title company may give you a reissue rate for title insurance. Your attorney may also receive discounts from a favorite title company.

- If your lender surprises you with a higher rate, more points, or additional fees, get an attorney involved or contact the lender's top management and your state's mortgage banker's association before the closing.

WHO WILL BE THERE?

At most closings, you will find these people:

- The buyer(s) and their attorney (if required) to sign documents and checks, and to protect the buyer's interests;

- The seller and his or her attorney (if required in your area);

- A settlement attorney may be used to coordinate some closings;

- The lender's representative is present to collect fees, make the loan, and protect the lender's interests;

- The title or escrow company representative is there to raise and help solve outstanding issues and collect any money for its account;

- The real estate broker(s) is there to collect the commission and help solve problems.

IT'S ALL YOURS!

The seller hands you the keys to your new home. Congratulations!

UNDERSTANDING EQUITY

When you're searching for a home to buy, you have to ask yourself if the property is worth the asking price. Even though selling a house you haven't yet bought is not uppermost in your mind, you want to be have the best opportunity to make a profit when you do sell the house.

STARTING EQUITY

Your equity is the difference between the remaining balance on your mortgage and the appraised value (expected selling price) of your home. For example, say you buy a $100,000 house. You make a down payment of $25,000 and borrow $75,000. You now have 25% equity in your home.

30 Most appraisals are good for six months.

RISING HOME VALUE INCREASES EQUITY

As the value of a home rises, the amount of equity in your home may increase. The value of a home can change almost immediately after you buy it. In fact, the actual price another buyer might be willing to pay for it immediately could be higher. Your home could also increase in value if:

- It has desirable features;
- It is in a desirable location;
- Home values, in general, rise;
- Inflation increases, causing home prices to rise along with it.

Of course, the value of a home can also fall, which would then decrease the amount of equity.

31 The market value is an estimate of the price you would receive if you sold your home.

LOWERING THE LOAN AMOUNT ALSO INCREASES EQUITY

As you repay your loan, the amount of equity will increase (unless the home's value decreases by a larger amount). If you have a negative amortization loan, you will actually have less equity as you make your payments (see pg. 43 for more details).

32 The faster you repay your loan, the faster your equity increases.

HOME EQUITY LOANS

Having equity in your home may give you the opportunity to access more money for your needs. You can obtain a home equity loan from a lender who thinks you have sufficient equity in your home to minimize the risk. The loan becomes a second mortgage and will be paid off when you sell your home, if you haven't paid it off before then. Home equity loans may be:

- A revolving line of credit, where you borrow money as you need it and pay it back as you would a credit card; or,
- A lump sum loan, where the lender gives you a lump sum which you can deposit in your account and pay back in regular monthly installments.

Some lenders require that you tell them what you will use the money for, others don't care. Check with your lender.

ENDING EQUITY

When you sell your house, the amount of equity you have is the selling price of the house minus the balance of your loan. The buyer's lender pays you that amount minus any commissions paid to the brokers or other fees associated with the sale of your home. You are then free to spend that money as you wish.

KEEPING INFORMED

Now that you are a homeowner, you have different responsibilities. One of the most important ones is keeping in touch with what is going on in your housing market. This will tell you what is happening with home values in your area, and may alert you to various opportunities.

INTEREST RATES

Experts suggest that if interest rates drop by more than two points, you might consider refinancing to lower your monthly payments. Before deciding, however, consider:

- Why you want to refinance;
- The interest rate of your mortgage;
- The interest rate of a new mortgage;
- The cost to refinance;
- How much equity you've built up in your home;
- Your current income and the quality of your credit record.

You may want to refinance to:

Receive a lower interest rate. You may find that you can get a new loan at a lower rate of interest, reducing your monthly payments. If you plan to remain in your home for several years, the savings could justify the costs of refinancing;

Build equity faster. By refinancing to a shorter-term mortgage, you can build equity faster, because a greater percentage of your monthly payment goes to the principal;

Switch from an adjustable to a fixed rate loan. Adjustable rate mortgages, traditionally offer lower interest rates during the early years of the loan than fixed rate loans. When rates drop, refinancing to a fixed rate loan, will give you a stable and predictable schedule of payments;

Switch from a fixed to an adjustable rate loan. An ARM may give you lower payments. Remember, however, that the interest rate on an ARM can increase at its periodic reset date, which means that your lower payment may only be for a limited time. If you only plan to live in your home for a short time, this switch may make sense;

Tap into your equity. Through what is often referred to as a *cash-out* refinance, you can tap the equity that has accumulated in your home to pay for expenses such as your children's education and home improvements.

TAKE IT ALL IN ▶
You may feel a little like this, considering all the information available. However, staying informed can make investing in a home a financially rewarding experience.

THE INTERNET

There are many websites that will provide information on homes in any area of the country or even, in some cases, the world. Some websites offer online tours so you can view a potential new home from the comfort of *your* home.

LOCAL NEWS

Pay attention to the local and national housing market changes, as well as their economy's. Businesses moving into areas may mean more jobs, which could raise demand for housing, driving home values up. Greater desirability for schools could also cause home prices to rise. Political events could change people's views about where the economy is going, which could have a ripple effect on home prices. Trends in the economy tend to have a great impact on housing prices.

YOUR BROKER

Keeping in touch with your broker can make you aware of trends in your neighborhood or another neighborhood you might consider in the future. Keeping your broker informed as your needs change may make your next home purchase smoother and easier.

ZONING LAWS

Housing areas are zoned for certain types of housing and/or businesses. Some areas can only have single-family houses, while others may allow apartment buildings and businesses. Zoning changes may affect the value of your home. You can find out about potential zoning changes through your local government. You may also have the power to stop certain changes by getting involved in your city's homeowner's association.

COMPARABLES

Keeping track of the comparables in your area after you have purchased a home will let you know which direction home values are headed.

INDEX

A
adjustable rate mortgages
  (ARMs), 40, 41
affording a home, 12–13
agents, 22–25, 55
amortization schedules, 55
Annual Percentage Rate (APR),
  37, 50
applications, 44–45, 54
appraisals, 49, 54
attorney fees, 55

B
balloon mortgages, 43
binding offers, 35
biweekly mortgage payments, 42
borrowers, 7
buy-downs, 43
buyer's agents, 25
buying versus renting, 8–9

C
cash
  finding, 12
  proof of, 44
casualty insurance, 58
catastrophic loss insurance, 59
checklists
  agent capabilities, 23
  buying a co-op, 29
closings, 62, 63
closing agents, 55
costs, 13, 55
commissions, 25
community property, 57
comparables, 26, 69
comparative market analysis, 33
condominiums, 28–29
contingency offers, 34
consumer organizations, 21
Consumer Price Index (CPI), 8
contracts
  exclusive, 25
  purchase, 35
conventional loans, 17
cooperatives (co-ops), 28–29, 59
costs
  additional mortgage, 54–55
  bounced check fees, 46
  closings, 13, 55

disclosing all, 50–51
extra, 37
good faith estimate, 49
hidden, 38
insurance, 58–59
of loans, 46
refinancing, 68
settlement, 49
subtracted from investment, 9
various related, 13
co-tenancy, 57
counteroffers, 34
covenants, conditions, and
  restrictions (CC&Rs), 28–29
credibility, 18–19
credit bureaus, 20
credit history, 15, 45
credit reports, 20–21, 54
credit unions, 38

D
debt, 12–13
deductible expenses, 11
defaulting on loans, 46, 47
Department of Housing and
  Urban Development (HUD), 39
deposits, 34
disadvantages of renting versus
  buying, 8–9
disclosures
  ARM documents, 41
  concealed information, 25
  by lenders, 19, 50–51
discrimination, 25
documents, 48–49, 64
downpayments, 12, 16
dual agents, 25
"due on sale" clauses, 57
dwelling types, 28–29, 31

E
earnest money, 34
Equifax, 20
equity
  building faster, 68
  growing equity mortgages, 42
  importance of to lenders, 15
  as resource, 13
  understanding, 66–67
expense to income ratio, 14

Experian, 20

F
Fannie Mae (FNMA), 7
Farmers Home Administration
  (FmHA), 39
Federal Housing Administration
  (FHA) loans, 17, 39
Federal Truth-in-Lending
  Disclosure Statement, 50
fees. See costs
15-year fixed rate loans, 53
finance charges, 50
financial assistance, 13
fixed rate mortgages, 40
foreclosures, 47
Freddie Mac (FHMC), 7

G
Genus Credit Management, 21
Ginnie Mae (GNMA), 7
Good Faith Estimates, 38
government fees, 55
government support, 10–11
graduated payments, 43

H
home equity loans, 67
home inspections, 54, 60–61
HUD settlement brochures, 48

I
illegal practices, 25
income, proof of your, 45
income taxes, 11
inspections, 55
insurance
  casualty, 58
  catastrophic loss, 59
  condominiums/co-ops, 59
  home warranties, 60
  liability, 59
  loss of use, 59
  mortgage, 13
  owner's title, 54
  personal injury, 59
  personal property, 58
  private mortgage insurance
    (PMI), 16–17
  on the structure, 58

title, 65
insurance companies, 38
interest, calculating, 52–53
interest, prepaying, 55
interest rates, 36–37, 40, 68
internet resources, 39, 52
investments, 9
investment values, 9
investors, large/small, 7

joint tenancy with rights of
  survivorship (JTWROS), 57

late charges, 50
late payments, 47
lenders
  direct, 38
  documents from, 48–49
  formulas used by, 14–15
  payments to, 55
  types of, 7
liability insurance, 59
living trusts, 57
loan amounts, 46
loan applications, 44–45
loan disclosures, 48
loan offers, 36–37
loan servicing transfers, 49
loan-to-value (LTV) ratios, 15
locked-in rates, 19
long-term debt, 14
loss of use insurance, 59
low income requirements, 17

M
median home prices, 26
monthly payments, 13
mortgage-backed securities, 7
mortgage bankers, 38
mortgage brokers, 39
mortgages
  adjustable rate (ARM), 41
  agreements, 46–47
  applications, 44–45
  balloon, 43
  biweekly, 42
  conventional, 17
  costs, 46, 54–55
  creative, 16
  defaulting on, 46, 47
  15-year fixed rate, 53
  fixed rate, 40
  growing equity, 42

home equity, 67
loan offers, 36–37
negative amortization, 43
"no doc," 42
non-conforming loans, 43
payments, types of, 43, 52–53
second, 67
switching types, 68
terms of, 37, 42
30-year fixed rate, 52
two-step, 42
types of payments, 52–53

N
negative amortization loans, 43
neighborhoods, researching, 27
"no doc" loans, 42
non-conforming loans, 43
non-discrimination notices, 48

O
offers
  binding, 35
  counteroffers, 34
  preparing, 32–33
  withdrawing, 35
ownership, 56, 57
owner's title insurance, 54

P
payments, 37, 50, 56
pay-offs, short, 46
personal injury insurance, 59
personal property insurance, 58
points, 10, 37
poor credit, 43
power of attorney, 62–63
prepaid finance charges, 51
prepayments, 46
prequalification, 18–19
principal, 46
private mortgage insurance
  (PMI), 16–17
purchase agreements, 28–29
purchase contracts, 35
purchase prices, 12, 26

R
rate caps, 41
rate lock-in, 48
refinancing, 68
renting versus buying, 8–9
repayment terms, 46
required deposits, 51
resale values, 27

S
saving money, 53
second mortgages, 67
self-employment issues, 15
sellers, 55
seller's subagents, 25
settlement costs, 49
short pay-offs, 46
short-term balloon mortgages, 43
sole ownership, 57
state programs, 39
structure insurance, 58
subsidies, government, 10
surveys, 54

T
taxes, 10, 11
teaser rates, 40
tenancy in common, 57
terms of loans, 37, 42, 47
third parties, 55
30-year fixed rate loans, 52
title insurance, 65
title searches, 54, 55
total sale price, 51
transaction brokers, 25
transfers of loan servicing, 49
Trans Union, 20
trusts, 57
Truth-in-Lending Disclosure
  Statement, 50
two-step mortgages, 42
types of homes, 28–29, 31
types of mortgage payments,
  52–53

U
umbrella liability insurance, 59
unconditional acceptances, 35

V
Veteran's Administration (VA)
  loans, 17, 39

W
walk-throughs, 63
websites, 20, 21
withdrawing offers, 35
withholdings, 11

Z
zoning laws, 69

ACKNOWLEDGMENTS

AUTHORS' ACKNOWLEDGMENTS

The production of this book has called on the skills of many people. We would like particularly to mention our editors at Dorling Kindersley, and our consultant, Nick Clemente. Marc wishes to dedicate this book to Zachary Robinson for his great patience and support when it was most needed.

PUBLISHER'S ACKNOWLEDGMENTS

Dorling Kindersley would like to thank everyone who generously lent props for the photo shoots, and the following for their help and participation:

Editorial Ruth Strother; Stephanie Rubenstein; **Design and Layout** Hedayat Sandjari; **Consultants** Nick Clemente; Skeeter; **Indexer** Rachel Rice; **Proofreader** Stephanie Rubenstein; **Photography** Anthony Nex; **Photographers' assistants** Damon Dumas; **Models** Joe Breckner; Ben Davis; Amanda Davis; **Picture researcher** Mark Dennis; Sam Ruston; **Additional photo credits:** Capitol building, pg. 39, Kevin Ryan; German red-roofed doll's house, pg. 60, Washington Dolls' Musuem

Special thanks to Teresa Clavasquin for her generous support and assistance.

AUTHORS' BIOGRAPHIES

Joe Breckner, GRI, has been a top producing real estate agent in the Los Angeles area for the past fifteen years. During that time Joe has participated in over 500 transactions totaling more than one hundred million dollars in sales production. Affiliated with Coldwell Banker, Joe is a member of the Presidents Elite, the top two percent of Coldwell Banker agents nationwide.

Marc Robinson is co-founder of Internet-based moneytours.com, a personal finance resource for corporations, universities, credit unions, and other institutions interested in helping their constituents make intelligent decisions about their financial lives. He wrote the original *The Wall Street Journal Guide to Understanding Money and Markets*, created *The Wall Street Journal Guide to Understanding Personal Finance*, co-published a personal finance series with Time Life Books, and wrote a children's book about onomateopia in different languages. In his two decades in the financial services industry, Marc has provided marketing consulting to many top Wall Street firms. He is admitted to practice law in New York State.